Edmund Carles Hopper

Some Account of the Parish of Starston, Norfolk

.

Edmund Carles Hopper

Some Account of the Parish of Starston, Norfolk

ISBN/EAN: 9783337410124

Printed in Europe, USA, Canada, Australia, Japan

Cover: Foto ©Lupo / pixelio.de

More available books at **www.hansebooks.com**

SOME ACCOUNT OF

THE

PARISH OF STARSTON,

NORFOLK,

COMPILED CHIEFLY FROM THE ANCIENT REGISTERS.

BY THE RECTOR

OF THE PARISH A.S. 1888.

NORWICH:

AGAS H. GOOSE AND CO., RAMPANT HORSE STREET.

1888.

TO MY DEAR WIFE.

PREFACE.

THERE is nothing very original, or I believe very particular about this history, which is almost entirely a collection of facts from the parish books. Most parishes have as much, many have more, facts of interest hidden away in their old books, to be brought to light by the first person who has leisure to do so.

I think I have acknowledged all obligations to other works ; but as I can but fear many mistakes may have been made, I shall consider it a favour if any friend will kindly be good enough to point them out to me.

E. C. H.

STARSTON.

OUR village of Starston is in the south-east of Norfolk, being eighteen miles south by east of Norwich, one mile from Harleston, ten from Diss, in the Diss or Southern Division of the county for electoral purposes, Harleston County Court and Petty Sessions Division, in the Rural Deanery of Redenhall, Archdeaconry of Norfolk, and Diocese of Norwich.

The bridge over the "beck" or stream that runs through the village, and empties itself into the Waveney just by Homersfield Bridge, is in longitude 1° 17″ east of Greenwich, 52° 31″ north latitude.

The name is probably Steers' Town, "the town of steers." In *Domesday Book* it is called Sterestuna ; and this must have been a common name for country villages in old times—for two certainly : Stuston near Diss, and Sturston near Thetford, also Tharston near Long Stratton probably, had originally the same name. Tharston, in old books, is sometimes written "Starston." They were all, I suppose, noted for cattle rearing in old times.

Its shape, as is so often the case in this district, is a long narrow strip of land, about four miles long, nearly five by road, and varying from about half-a-mile in the north to more than a mile on the south in breadth. It is bounded on the north by Hardwick ; east, by Redenhall with Harleston ; south, by Needham ; west, by Pulham S. Mary the Virgin.

When *Domesday Book* was written, shortly before 1086 A.D., "Sterestuna" was a village one mile five furlongs long, and five furlongs broad. Perhaps, in those days, only the strip from the village to Starston Hall was cultivated. In those days the parish paid 13*d.* "geld." Its present acreage is 2244, which is four acres over three and a half square miles ; and the rateable value in 1875 was £3503.

The population in 1698 was 215 ;

in 1798   385 :

96 men, 125 women, 82 girls and 82 boys under fifteen.   In 1871 it was 495 ;

1881   510.

Last year, when an informal census was taken for the purpose of the fête at the Queen's Jubilee, it was found that there were over 530 inhabitants—in all, I think, about 545.

THE CHURCH,

Dedicated to S. Margaret, stands on the brow of the hill just north of the bridge. When the original Starston church was built I am unable now to say. The south wall of the present nave is Norman, and is not later than A.D. 1150—1200.

Whether any earlier church existed on the same spot in old times I do not know; the south wall is, at any rate, the oldest part of the present building. If you will look at the south wall (outside), between the porch and the nearest south window, you will see where an old round-headed (Norman) window has been—but is now filled up. There is a similar filled-up window further east, covered now by the creepers.

There are no windows of that date in use now, unless a conjecture of my own be correct, viz., that the east belfry window is really one of the earlier tower windows, inserted in the tower when rebuilt. It might be, from its shape, a restored Norman or early English window : it is certainly strange that the four are not alike.

The church walls (nave) and the tower were raised to their present height, and the present windows inserted, *about* 1300 ; the chancel and chancel arch may be also of this date.

It is said that the old chancel was longer than the present one, extending further east : this may be so, but I do not know that there is any proof of this.

The churchyard is oa. 3r. 27p. It is possible that the church pightle was in ancient times also church-yard.

The roof of the church is a very good specimen of Perpendicular work. It is of plain arch-brace construction, without hammer or collar beams. It was almost entirely renewed in 1870, but on the original designs. It was formerly painted over with what were thought to be white stars : I think, perhaps, that they were intended for ox-eye daisies (Margaret daisies), after the patron saint of the church.

The arch between the tower and the church is more lofty than usual, which adds much to the light and ventilation.

Behind the pulpit there is, as so often in old churches, the rood staircase. So far as is known, in ancient times the priest used to ascend this staircase on great festivals, and lifted up a cross on the rood-screen for adoration. Rood-screens still remain in many churches : the best specimen in this district being that in Eye church. Others are in Pulham S. Mary and Hardwick.

The hinges on the principal door are fine speci-mens of ancient blacksmith's work. In this case they are real hinges : not, as more usually, mere ornamentation.

The font is large, as all old fonts were—sufficient to totally immerse an infant, if necessary.

None of the windows call for any special remark. The best, I think, is the aisle window, west side; the east window is poor. All are of Perpendicular work. There are two good memorial windows in the chancel.

✝

CHURCH FURNITURE.

The present altar was made in 1847, by Rattee of Cambridge. In the front is an old carving (probably of the sixteenth century) of the Lord's Supper, which was accidentally obtained by Archdeacon Hopper at a sale.

The old altar, probably the original Elizabethan "communion table," placed in the church at the Reformation, was not destroyed, but is used as a vestry table.

The expense of the new altar (1847) was defrayed by my aunt, Mrs. Russell Apletre of Goldings, Basingstoke, Hants.

The altar rails were made at the same time, at the expense of Miss M. A. F. Hopper of Leeds. The old rails are still used in the gallery.

The vestry was built at the same time, and the entire chancel reseated and restored, at the private expense (£250) of Archdeacon Hopper.

The pulpit, (wooden) lectern, and reading desk

were carved by Rattee, and were erected at the private expense of Archdeacon Hopper in 1854. The panels of the pulpit are parts of an ancient screen.

The velvet altar cover was worked by Miss Charlotte Holmes of Gawdy Hall, in 1847.

In 1856 the nave was thoroughly restored and reseated with the present oak benches, and the floor paved with encaustic tiles, at the cost of £338. 4s. 10d., defrayed by Archdeacon Hopper.

In 1870, the church being found too small for the congregation, a north aisle was built, with organ chamber, and the roof almost rebuilt, at the cost of £978. 5s. 9d. At the same time the west gallery (except that part within the tower) was removed, allowing the light of the west window to enter the church.

In 1878 the organ was rebuilt, and a brass eagle lectern presented, in memorial of the late Archdeacon Hopper, by his four children.

In 1883 the lych-gate was built, at the sole expense of Mrs. Hopper. The design follows the lych-gate at Denton, which was in part designed by Archdeacon Hopper.

The church now has 245 sittings.

THE BELLS.

There are five bells in the tower, the inscriptions on them being as follows :—

1.—" C. & G. Mears, Founders, London, MDCCCXLVII."

2.—" Anno Domini 1619." On crown three shields : one of Norwich city arms, one of the Brasyer family, and one "$^{A}_{W}{}^{B}$."

3.—" C. & G. Mears, Founders, London, 1847."

4.—" C. & G. Mears, Founders, London. Augustus Macdonald Hopper, Rector. Charles Etheredge, David Feaveryer, Churchwardens, 1847."

5.—Same as 2.

The diameters are 26, 27½, 30, 32, and 36 inches ; their weight, approximately, 4, 5, 6, 7, and 9 cwts.

In the inventory of the 6th year of Edward VI. there were four bells here, weighing 6, 7, 9, and 11 cwts. The peal was evidently made five in 1619, when the present 2 and 5 were cast. These bells were cast by William Brend of Norwich, whose initials, with those of his wife (Alice Brend), are on a shield on the crown of the bells. Other bells by Brend in this neighbourhood are—the treble at Denton (1616), the second at Pulham S. Mary (1611), and the fifth at Mendham (1623).

One bell, which is not mentioned, was recast at Norwich in 1723 (see churchwardens' accounts); and when Blomefield wrote his history in 1750

he mentions that the inscription on the fifth was—
" Nos, Thome meritis, mereamur gaudia lucis " (may
we, by the merits of Thomas, deserve the joys of
light). The old peal of five have the tradition
of being a fine ring of bells, and the churchwardens'
accounts often contain items of gifts to the ringers—
generally 5s. or 10s., at "ye powder plot" and
other times.

By 1847, however, the bells were in sad plight :
the tenor was broken, the 2 and 3 cracked, and only
the 1 and 4 whole, so the three broken bells were
recast ; but by an unfortunate mistake, not for their
original position, but into the present 1, 3, 4.   Of
course the sale of some six cwt. of bell metal made
the bell-founder's bill less, but it spoilt the peal,
since the present second (the old treble), though a
good treble bell, is not so well suited for a second.
The present tenor has been a very fine bell, but
must have lost much of its power by being chipped
to bring it into tune with the others.   It is still the
best bell of the peal ; the fourth and then the treble
being the worst.

Before the Reformation all bells were dedicated
to some saint, generally the favourite saint of the
time, thus our old tenor bell was dedicated to
S. Thomas.   It is said that the tenor bell was
always dedicated to the patron saint of the church :
except in two cases I can find no instance of this.
At Redenhall, both church and tenor bell are dedicated to S. Mary ; at Metfield, both to S. John the
Baptist.   It is usually some other saint.

I have not been able to find out the inscriptions on the old 2 and 3 bells; but as one was recast in Norwich in 1723, we may infer that the founder was Thomas Newman, who recast the Pulham S. Mary tenor in 1739; or John Stephens, who cast the peal of six at Pulham Market.*

THE ORGAN.

In old times I do not think there was often any fixed instrument in our churches. Village music was performed by professors on the clarionet, flute, key bugle, violin, or 'cello, and I can only regret that so little interest is taken in these things now. Why should we not be able to have a village band? If they could do these things fifty or a hundred years ago, we ought to be able to do better, with all our advantages. There is an entry in the church-wardens' accounts for payment to the "Alburgh singers:" no doubt, one of those local bands who used to perform "dirges" on solemn occasions.

Isaac Kent is our first performer of whom, so far as I know, any traditions remain. Besides being parish clerk, he played on the flute in church.

In 1838 Mr. Spencer gave a barrel organ to the

* See L'Estrange's *Church Bells of Norfolk.*

church : there were, I think, four barrels, and ten tunes on each barrel. This is still at Needham church.

In 1864 Mrs. Holmes of Gawdy Hall gave us a small organ, consisting of but one stop, with an octave coupler (open diapason to tenor C, with a stopped bass), built by Holditch. To this a dulciana to tenor C and an octave of bourdon pedals were added, in which state the organ remained till 1878, when it was entirely rebuilt by Rayson of Ipswich, who, however, used all the old pipes and such parts of the case as were available. The tracker work and all the mechanism were, however, entirely new. It now consists of two complete manuals, C C to G, 56 notes, and pedal organ, C C C to E, 29 notes, and the following stops :—

GREAT ORGAN.

1.—Open Diapason, metal	-	-	8 ft.	56 pipes.
2.—Stopt Diapason, wood	-	-	8 ,,	56 ,,
3.—Dulciana, metal (grooved into 2)			8 ,,	44 ,,
4.—Principal, metal	-	-	-	4 ,,	56 ,,
5.—Flute, open wood	-	-	-	4 ,,	56 ,,
6.—Cremona, spotted metal	-	-	8 ,,	44 ,,

SWELL ORGAN.

1.—Open Diapason (grooved into 2)		8 ,,	44 ,,
2.—Lieblich Gedact, oak	-	-	8 ,,	56 ,,
3.—Principal, metal	-	-	-	4 ,,	56 ,,
4.—Fifteenth, metal	-	-	-	2 ,,	56 ,,
5.—Oboe, spotted metal	-	-	-	8 ,,	56 ,,

PEDAL ORGAN.

1.—Bourdon - - - - - 16 ft. 29 pipes.
2.—Octave, open wood - - - 8 „ 29 „

COUPLERS.

1.—Swell to great.
2.—Swell to pedals.
3.—Great to pedals.

Two combination pedals to the great organ.
One   „   „   swell.

Total : 16 stops and 638 pipes.

MONUMENTS IN STARSTON CHURCH.

Of these, the most interesting is that to the memory of Bartholomew Cotton, on the north side of the chancel. It is rather an elaborate piece of work, in marble of various colours, Mr. Cotton being represented kneeling at a reading desk, in gown and ruff of the period. The inscription below is :—

" Hic in Christo obdormit Bartholomeus Cotton Armiger filius et Hæres Rogeri Cotton ex antiqua familia Cottonorum de Landwade in Comitatu Cantabrigiæ per Etheldredam filiam et hæredem Johannis Cotton fratris

secundi Rob⁹ti Cotton de Landwade Militis Qui veræ
religionis verus Cultor beneficus egenis et omnibus Charus
munere eirenarchæ complures annos et clerici brevium
atque processuum in camera stellata XXXIII annos cum
summa integritatis laude perfunctus.

"Tres duxit uxores Ceciliam Burrough virginem et
hæredem Aliciam Gascoigne et Annam Sterlinge viduas
animam deo pie et placide reddidit, die lunæ, viz., XXI
Junii, anno salutis MDCXIII Aetatis suæ LXXVI.

"Patri Optimo Thomas filius et hæres in officio
Successor observantiæ ergo posuit."

Here sleeps in Christ, Bartholomew Cotton, Knt., son
and heir of Roger Cotton, of the ancient family of the
Cottons of Landwade, in the county of Cambridge, by
Etheldreda, daughter and heiress of John Cotton, second
brother of Robert Cotton of Landwade, soldier (Esquire :)
who, being a true promoter of the true religion, beneficent
to the needy, and charitable to all, performed, with the
highest praise of integrity, the duty of an eirenarch (Justice
of Peace) for many years, and for thirty-three years the
office of a member of the Star Chamber, and Clerk of
Briefs.

He married three wives, Cecilia Burrough, spinster and
heiress; Alice Gascoigne and Anna Sterlinge, widows.

He piously and calmly gave up his soul to God on the
21 day of the month June, in the year of grace 1613, and
of his age 76.

To his most excellent father, Thomas, his son and heir,
by duty of being his successor, placed this to his memory.

Bartholomew Cotton, consequently, was born in
1537.

Register of Burials, 1613 :—" Mr. Bartholomew Cotton Esquiour was buried. June 23rd."

In the aisle are monuments to Mr. Arrowsmith, thirty years rector of this parish and Alburgh ; and to a Mr. Robert Ferrier, of whom I know no further particulars.

TOMBSTONES WITHIN THE CHURCH.

1.—Within the Altar Rails, south end :—

Beneath are deposited
The remains of
Mrs. Margaret Arrowsmith,
Who departed this life
May 4th, 1761,
Aged 88 years.

2.—Under the Altar, a little to the north :—

Here lyeth interr'd the body of Anna Cotton, late wife of Luckin Cotton, Esqr, who departed this life the eighth day of August, 1658.

3.—Under the Cotton monument :—

Arms of Cotton.

> Here lie the bodies together of Luckin
> Cotton, Gent. (who, being about 25 yeares of age)
> was interr'd Jan. ye 17, 1654, and of his two
> infant sonnes Luckin and Bartholomew, who
> (like untimely fruit) fell all at a blast, and in
> ye space of ten months, withered away in ye immaturity
> of their years. Bartholomew (being about a yeare old)
> was buried April ye 13th, 1655 ; and Luckin y^e
> eldest sonne, not being 3 years old, periodized y^e
> males of his family here by his deplored death, & was
> buried October ye 3rd, 1655.

Our happiest dayes doe passe from vs poor mortalle men
first and before the rest.—SENECA.

4.—Just within the south chancel door, is a stone
with this legend :—

> Here lyeth the body of Philip, the sonne of
> Francis Bacon, Esq., and Dorothy his wife, who
> died unweaned at Nurse, and was buried 21
> day of November, 1657.

Death is the sentence of the Lord over all flesh.

[This inscription is preserved by Blomefield. It
is almost illegible on the slab.]

5.—On a large slab just within the great door is a small brass with this legend :—

Here lyeth William Bagott, gentleman, who departed the 4th day of November, & buryed ye 8th daye, A^o dni. 1580.

Blessed is he that dyeth with the Lord.

6.—In the vestry hangs a hatchment with this legend :—

Arms of Cotton.

In memory of Luckin Cotton, gent, interr'd Jan. ye 17, 1654. He left two sonnes, Luckin & Bartholomew, & 2 Daughters, Lidia & Mary. Barth. & Luckin dyed since, & were buryed by their ffather, Barth, April ye 14, & Luckin, October the 3, 1655.

In the year 1870 the north wall of the nave was pulled down, in order to build the new aisle. In removing the plaster an arched recess was discovered, about the middle of the wall, and two feet from the ground ; it was about four feet in height and the same in width. It had, perhaps, been bricked up since the Reformation.

This niche was about a foot deep, and contained a mural painting, supposed to represent the death of the Blessed Virgin. As good a copy as possible was taken at the time by Mr. Phipson, the architect, and was lithographed by the Norfolk Archæological Society. The date of the painting is supposed to be about the end of the thirteenth century.

VESSELS FOR THE HOLY COMMUNION.

1.—One chalice and cover, which may be used as a paten.

This was the private property of Archbishop Sancroft, and is one of the treasures of the parish. Back to 1742 it has belonged to us, and from 1742 to 1687 it was doubtless in possession of the Sancroft family.

I hope to find out, some day, the history of this chalice from 1567 to 1687, the question being whether it was merely bought by Archbishop Sancroft, i.e., whether it has any particular history or not. Dr. Raven, the present vicar of Fressing-field, does not know that it has any connection with that parish, and some passages in D'Oyly's *Life of Sancroft* make me think that it more probably came from Lambeth ; especially as parochial chalices are usually, though not always, inscribed with the name of the parish (*vide infra*.)

I subjoin part of a letter copied verbatim from D'Oyly's *Life*, which shows us something of the Archbishop's mind; also a list, taken from an article in the Norfolk and Norwich Archæological Society's Papers (vol. ix., part 1) by the Rev. C. R. Manning of Diss, of other Elizabethan communion plate in this deanery alone.

2.—One small paten. Also the property of Archbishop Sancroft; date about 1691.

3.—One larger paten.
"S. Deo et Ecclesiæ de Starston in Com. Norf. 1721."

4.—One larger paten, given by Archdeacon Hopper about 1870.
" Lord, evermore give us this bread."
In the centre the Paschal Lamb.

5.—One larger chalice.
" Deo servatori sacrum.
Eccl. de Starston in Com. Norff."
On the other side—I H S, surrounded by a nimbus; date 1691.

6.—One flagon.
"Ecclesiæ de Starston, dedit M. A. F. Hopper, 1847."

7.—One alms dish of bronze.
One alms dish of oak.
One alms dish of pewter.

C

[I generally use Archbishop Sancroft's chalice at all services, also the flagon; and paten No. 2 for early services, No. 3 for mid-day celebrations of the Holy Communion.]

In this deanery alone the following chalices are of the date 1567 :—Bressingham, Dickleburgh (*circa*), Earsham, Gissing, Pulham S. Mary Magdalen, Starston, Winfarthing; while one at Diss is of the date 1564.

There are also " Elizabethan " vessels at Billingford, Denton, and eight other parishes.

Of these, the following have the name of the parish inscribed on them :—Bressingham, Dickleburgh, Earsham, Gissing, both Pulhams, and the two Tivetshalls.

My own query is whether the absence of the name of the parish on our chalice suggests that it was not originally a " parochial " chalice at all. Vessels at Needham, Rushall, &c., though in all probability Elizabethan, have not, however, the name of the parish inscribed.

GENEALOGY OF THE SANCROFT FAMILY.

A genealogy, showing the connection of four Starston families with the Archbishop :—

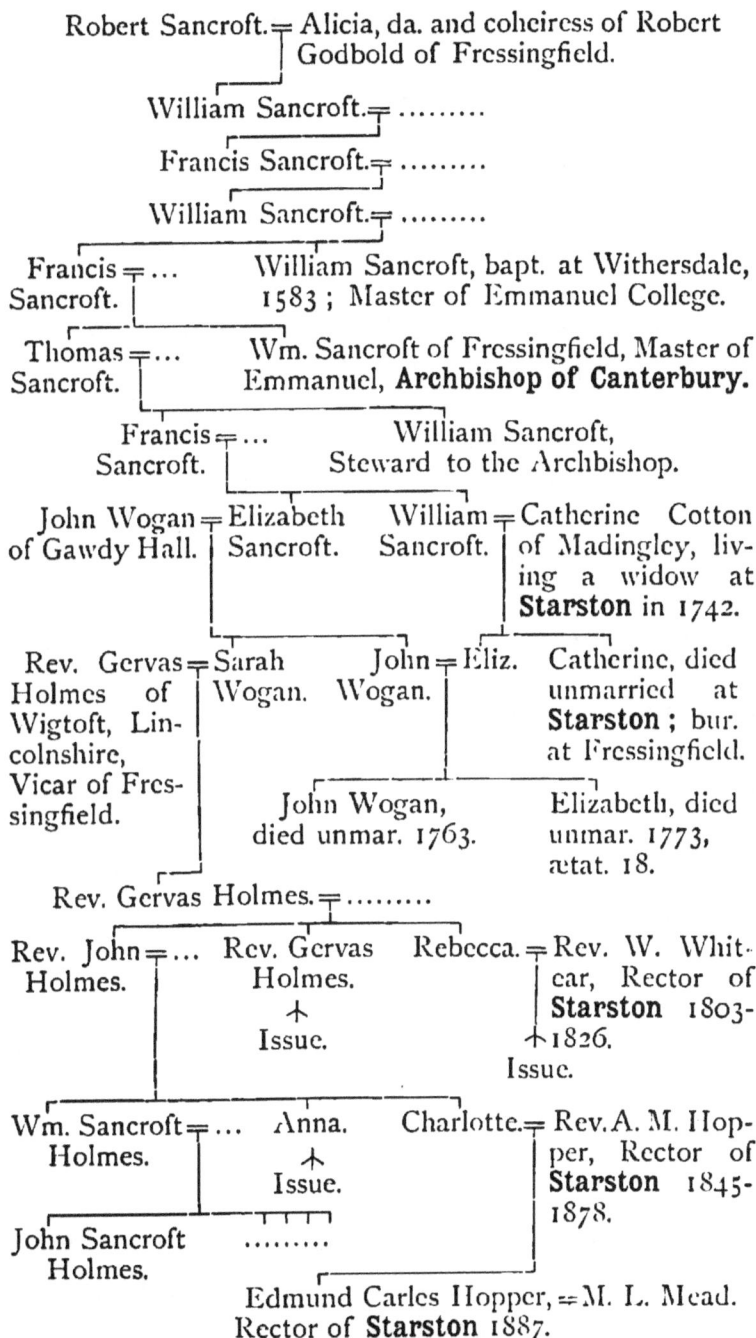

Robert Sancroft.=Alicia, da. and coheiress of Robert
Godbold of Fressingfield.

William Sancroft.=.........

Francis Sancroft.=.........

William Sancroft.=.........

Francis=...   William Sancroft, bapt. at Withersdale,
Sancroft.   1583 ; Master of Emmanuel College.

Thomas=...   Wm. Sancroft of Fressingfield, Master of
Sancroft.   Emmanuel, **Archbishop of Canterbury.**

Francis=...   William Sancroft,
Sancroft.   Steward to the Archbishop.

John Wogan=Elizabeth   William=Catherine Cotton
of Gawdy Hall. Sancroft. Sancroft. of Madingley, liv-
                                  ing a widow at
                                  Starston in 1742.

Rev. Gervas=Sarah   John=Eliz.   Catherine, died
Holmes of Wogan. Wogan.   unmarried at
Wigtoft, Lin-   **Starston** ; bur.
colnshire,   at Fressingfield.
Vicar of Fres-
singfield.   John Wogan,   Elizabeth, died
                    died unmar. 1763.   unmar. 1773,
                                        ætat. 18.

Rev. Gervas Holmes.=.........

Rev. John=...   Rev. Gervas   Rebecca.=Rev. W. Whit-
Holmes.   Holmes.   car, Rector of
                ⋏   **Starston** 1803-
                Issue.   ⋏1826.
                                        Issue.

Wm. Sancroft=...   Anna.   Charlotte.=Rev.A. M. Hop-
Holmes.   ⋏   per, Rector of
                   Issue.   **Starston** 1845-
                                       1878.
John Sancroft   ....
Holmes.

                    Edmund Carles Hopper, =M. L. Mead.
                    Rector of **Starston** 1887.

" Fresingfield,

" December 23rd, 1691.

" Honest, constant, dear friend,

" I write this only to present my kindest respects to my noble friend, your landlord, and yourself; and to let you know (seeing you so kindly inquire after it) that I bless God I am well, at the old rate, which you know, and have been so (without the interruption of single day), ever since I came to this place. But the spirit of calumny, the persecution of the tongue, dogs me, even into this wilderness. Dr. Lake, of Garlic Hill, and others, have (as I am informed), filled your city with a report that I go constantly to this parish church, and pray for I know not whom, nor how, and receive the holy sacrament there ; so that my cousin had something to do to satisfy even my friends that it was quite otherwise : whereas I was never so much as once out of this poor house, and the yards and avenues, since I came first directly from London into it ; and I never suffered our vicar, or any other, nor even my chaplains, when they were here, so much as say grace where I eat ; but I constantly officiate myself *secundum usum Lambethenum*, which you know, and never give the holy sacrament but to those of my own persuasion and practice ....

" Yours, yours,

"W. C."

PATRONAGE OF THE LIVING.

The present Rector is the patron of the living of Starston ; but he must present it to a Fellow of S. John's College, Cambridge.

The history of this somewhat unusual arrangement is as follows :—

When Henry VIII., though unwilling that the Pope of Rome should have any power in England, yet reserved nearly all his authority to himself, he gave to his favourites and others all the ecclesiastical property he could lay his hands on : this is the reason that so many benefices are still what are called vicarages, the great tithes belonging to some layman, or other body not connected with the parish.

By a deed of the 28th year of Henry VIII. (1537) the King granted to Robert, Earl of Sussex, the rectory and advowson of Starston and Hempnall, after which it passed through various hands to the Hon. and Rev. Richard Hill, who was a Fellow of S. John's College, Cambridge. This person, by deed dated 23rd November, 1723, settled the advowson of Alburgh, Ditchingham, North and South Lopham, Forncett S. Mary and S. Peter, and Starston, on his own family, provided they only appointed Fellows of S. John's College, Cambridge. In 1802 a member of the Hill family sold all these advowsons to the Duke of Norfolk, subject, however, to the previous limitation ; and although the advowson of some of these livings has since changed hands, the first offer of them all must still be made to the Fellows of S. John's College, Cambridge. It was only on the refusal of all of them to accept it, after Mr.

Watson's resignation, that I was able to appoint myself.

It appears from Blomefield that the patron had always been some member of a Norfolk family.

THE RECTORY

Is so far interesting as being one of the oldest rectory-houses in this neighbourhood.   It was built by the Rev. Richard Anguish, Rector of Starston 1637-1644, in which year he was turned out of this house by Cromwell's soldiers.   The present front of this house, consisting of two rooms on the ground floor, two rooms on the first floor, and the attics, remained very much as he built them, and as they are now, till Mr. Whitear's time.   Miss Whitear informs me that when her father came to this parish in 1803 he was informed that "there was a very good rectory-house at Starston : there are two good rooms *and a pump.*"   There is still remaining the little sketch Mr. Whitear sent to his father of the house, in which the pump certainly holds a somewhat prominent position, being in the front drive.

Mr. Whitear built the study and two rooms over it.

Mr. Spencer built the drawing-room and rooms over, with the kitchen.

Archdeacon Hopper built the parish-room, the nurseries, the front porch; he bought and pulled down the house where Archdeacon Oldershaw used to live, using, however, his stables and out-buildings; and he pulled down the old rectory stables, which stood east of the rectory, where the present tennis ground is. He also made many alterations of glebe, &c., too numerous to mention, but certainly all to the advantage of the rectory.

The commutation price value of the living is £663, with rectory and (now) twenty-two acres of glebe. Old terriers seem to imply that there was formerly much more glebe than now.

Until quite lately every parish used to provide for its own poor. The Starston "town-house" used to stand where the church pightle now is; then three houses on the Pulham road were built, of which a full account is in the churchwardens' books for the year 1828. These houses (the stone cottages) were bought by Mr. Taylor when the Union-house at Pulham was built, and several parishes joined to form one common "union."

The bridge over the stream was built in 1825 by John Brown, the county architect. On the east side is " J. B., 1825." Before that time there was only a ford and a foot bridge.

Starston Hall has been a good specimen of a country manor-house: a moat used to protect it from all robbers and other inconvenient people. When it was rebuilt a few years ago, care was taken to keep the fine old chimneys in their original pattern.

The railway was made through the village in 1856, and there was a small station here till 1866, when it was closed, and there is now only a level crossing.

THE ANCIENT MANORS OF STARSTON.

The old division of the country into manors is a thing now well-nigh forgotten, and out of date ; but a hundred years ago, as, for instance, when Blomefield wrote, it was the chief item of local interest. It is a relic of the old feudal system, which partly remains in the word " copy " hold.

The old manors were five in number—Starston Hall, Bresingham's, Beckhall, Bolton's, and Gunshaw :—

Starston Hall.—This manor was owned about A.D. 1300 by the Bagot family (this name is variously spelled Pygot, Pycot, &c.), and though a detailed account is given in Blomefield, it is not, I think, necessary to transcribe the various owners who bought and sold it. It seems, however, chiefly to have remained in the Bagot family.

Bresingham's Manor, Starston Place, was, from 1235 to 1462, in the possession of the Bresingham family, who, no doubt, came from the village of that name, beyond Diss. It was then bought by the Pigots or Bagots, and William Bagot sold it in 1578 to Bartholomew Cotton—both of whom are buried inside the church (see Monuments.)

Beckhall Manor, Mr. Palmer's farm-house, though demolished in Blomefield's time, stood near the present house, and from 1296-1358 it belonged to the Ingham family, after which it was frequently bought and sold, and finally passed through the hands of the Gawdy family to the *Cottons*, who united it to Bresingham's manor.

Bolton's Manor is not really in this parish, but in Pulham, at the extreme north end, on the borders of Starston and Hardwick. There is still the moat and island where the house stood, and it may have extended to the farm where Mr. Riches now lives, which is called Bolton's Manor Farm. It was, at one time, in the possession of Sir Peter Gleane.

Gunshaw's Manor is in this parish and Needham, the boundary running through the house; but it usually is considered as belonging to Needham. It seems, like Needham, to have had ancient connections with Mendham Priory.

The boundary between this parish and Needham goes through the oven; and the old joke was to bake a cake in the oven, on days when they beat the bounds, and to send a boy into the oven to get it.

STARSTON PLACE.

Since this house was known as Bresingham's manor it belonged to the Cotton family, from 1578 till soon after 1742, for it was no doubt in her own or her own family's right that Mrs. Catherine Sancroft (*née* Cotton) and her daughter lived here in 1742. We have already seen that that family left no remaining issue.

When Blomefield wrote, Mr. Waldegrave Pelham was owner and occupier.

In 1824 the owner was General Clay; but the occupier was Mr. Thomas L. Lingwood, for many years Churchwarden. It was then sold to Mr. Taylor of Diss, who established the *model farm*, still in the possession of his family.

So much of the parish being well cultivated and cared for, the cottages properly built and kept up, are things which have always tended to the prosperity of the parish.

Other good houses in the parish are Grove Hill, built in 1849, and Conifer Hill, built in 1881.

REGISTERS.

From the ancient registers of the parish I have copied the following items, as unusually worthy of notice :—

On the fly-leaf, in the handwriting of Peter Raye :—

Memento te esse mortalem
Nascimur morituri morimur victuri
Bene vivere est bis vivere
Semper ita vivendum ut rationem nobis reddendam arbitremur
Christus in vita et morte mihi unicum lucrum.

P. R.

Crux Christi scala cœli
Crux
Tho. Fuller.

Bis vincit qui vincit in victoria.

On the following page is a complete list of the Rectors of Starston till the present date :—

John Mutlow, 1552-1553.

Thomas Palmer, Rector of Starston, buried 3rd January, 1575.

Peter Raye, Rector of Starston 1558-1611.

George Ray, Rector of Starston 1611-1623.

> Then held by Curates till 1637.

Richard Anguise, Rector 1637-1644, when he was turned out by Cromwell's soldiers, after building the front of the house. (See Rectory.)

Mr. Fisher, Minister of Starston, 1659.

Mr. Christopher Spendlove, Minister of Starston five years, 1661-1666.

Mr. Richard Luthwit, Minister of Starston four years.

Cuthbert Browne, December, 1672.

William Wiat, September 29th, 1679.

Thomas Arrowsmith, September 29th, 1699.

Philip Williams, August, 1729.

George Davies, February 12th, 1746-7.

Thomas Frampton, October, 1768.

William Whitear, November 16th, 1803.

William Pakenham Spencer, instituted May 9th, 1827.

Augustus Macdonald Hopper, instituted October 24th, 1845.

Frederick Watson, instituted June 18th, 1878.

Edmund Carles Hopper, instituted April 2nd, 1887.

BLOMEFIELD'S LIST OF THE RECTORS OF STARSTON.

1306. Robert de Beverley, resigned.

1319. John Pikard of Hardwick.

1348. John Woodward.

1361. Will. Danyel.

1372. Tho. de Trowel, resigned.

1379. John Haselore.

1383. Tho. Alborn, resigned.

1386. John Gelle, resigned.

1393. John Lese.

1408. Will. Newton.

(?) Will. Baker, resigned.

1420. Alex. Colloo, died the next year and was buried here.

1421. John Wele, resigned.

1437. John Swan, died in 1478, buried in the chancel.

1478. Peter Wodecock.

1515. Nich. Carr.

1531. Nic. Cotney.

1558. Will. Clark, resigned same year.

1558. Thomas Palmer.

1576. George Grame.

1586. Peter Raye.

1603. Peter Rix.

1629. Will. Bennett.

1638. Ric. Anguish.

1669. Ric. Lewthwaite.

1672. Will. Wyatt.

1699. Tho. Arrowsmith.

1725. Philip Williams.

1746. George Davies.

It is evident that one or other of these lists is slightly inaccurate. They will, however, fit together, if we take Blomefield's list till 1558, and the register list from 1746, and make the following notes between 1558 and 1746:—

Peter Raye was not *Rector* till 1586, but he seems to have written all the early parts of the Register himself, probably copied from some older register, now long since lost ; and his signature must be taken as that of the copyist, not as having performed the ceremonies. He is mentioned by Blomefield as being also Rector of Stratton S. Peter, but the dates, if so, are incorrect.

Peter Rix, } These two are not mentioned in our
Will. Bennett, } registers, except as Curates.

Mr. Fisher, }
C. Spendlove, } These are not mentioned by Blomefield,
C. Browne, } but are mentioned in the registers.

Philip Williams was the first presented by S. John's College. He was Rector also of *Barrow* in Suffolk, another Johnian living ; he resigned, but was still alive when Blomefield wrote.

From the "towne book" we find that the sequestrator of the living was one Robert Kent, who is called "Robert Kent, clarke," in the overseers' accounts for three or four years. He may have been the Presbyterian Minister thrust in to replace Anguish. His successor, Thomas Fisher, from the same book, was in possession here till 1660.

Of this list of Rectors, William Wiat, and Thomas Arrowsmith certainly, and C. Spendlove, probably were also Rectors of the adjoining parish of Alburgh, as appears by the registers of that parish. Several other of our Rectors seem to have done occasional or even regular duty there. Of the names appearing in our registers, Fairfax Stillingfleet, who seems to have lived at Syleham, was Curate of both parishes, then Rector of Alburgh. John Malyn and David Anthony Heck were also Curates of both parishes.

We certainly have not suffered so much by the non-residence of the Rectors at Starston as most parishes have. From 1623-1644 there were only Curates here, and no Rector's name appears in the "Towne booke," although names are given by Blomefield, who, however, is not always accurate. Even during the Commonwealth there were two clergy; but probably from the state of the registers they were either Presbyterian or other Nonconformist partisans of the parliament. Philip Williams seems to have given up the care of his parish a good deal to F. Stillingfleet; and for the last fourteen years Dr. Frampton was absent at Newmarket, where he died, and is, I believe, buried.

Beyond this, I can find *no* evidence of non-residence in Starston.

Other memoranda to be gathered from Blomefield are :—

In 1603, when the Communion was compulsory, there were 120 Communicants here.

In the King's Books the Rectory is valued at £15, and the yearly tenths as £1. 10s.

1740. Thomas Aldous, a poor man, buried, aged 106 years.

A true Register of all the Christinninges, Mariages, and Burialls, that have beene in this towne of Starston, from the first yeere of the raygne of our soveraine Lady Queene Elizabeth, anno domini 1558. Petro Raye, rectore.

Imprimis William, the sonne of William Reade, was baptised the xxii daye of September, 1558.

Hester, ye daughter of Thomas Palmer, clarke, was bap. 1 August.

Nathaniell, ye sonne of Thomas Palmer, was bap. 19 January (and 3 more children.)

1575. Thomas Palmer, Clarke, Rector of Starston, was buried ye 3rd daye of January.

1586. Margarett, ye daughter of Peter Raye, clarke, was bap. November 26, (and several more.)

1596. Mr. John Gascoigne and Mrs. Judith Cotton were maryed Sep. 14.

1603. The Ladye Bowes buryed the 7th of August.

1613. Mr. Bartholomew Cotton, esquire, was buried June 23.

1626. Mr. Thomas Cotton, esquier, was buried the 5th of May.

1628. A man childe of Bartholomew Cotton, Esquier, was buried the 29 of January.

1630. Luckin, the son of Barth. Cotton, Esqr. and Jane his wife, was bapt. June the 10th.
Richard, the son of Barth. Cotton, Esqr., and Jane his wife, was bapt. Febru. the 24th (buried next day), (and other children.)

1634. Barthew. Cotton, Esqr. buryed July 13th.

1639. Ann, the daughter of Ric. Anguise, rector, and Katherine his wife, was baptised Dec. 17, 1639 (and others.)

It seems that during the Commonwealth births were inserted, but baptisms forbidden. During ten years there are very few entries, of which the following are fair specimens :—

1649. Ann, the daughter of Daniel Androus, was borne the 3 day of August, 1649.

1660. Eliz., the daughter of Patyc Garmin, was bounc the 11 day of March, 1660. [I cannot quite make out this name: there are several more children of the same parent mentioned].

[Registers filled in, it seems, by returned Rectors.]

1649. James Haylocke, the sonne of Edmund Haylocke and Ann his wife, was ~~baptised~~ borne December the 30, 1649.

1656. Mary Richards, the daughter of Daniel Richards and Mary his wife, was born 11 February, 1656, and was baptised the 3 July, 1662.

1688. Thomas, the sonne of William Wiat, Rector, and Hannah his wife, was born the nineteenth day, and baptised the twenty-seventh day of September, 1688.

1699. Mr. William Wyatt, late Rector of Starston, buried September 30, 1699.

1704. Thomas Arrowsmith, Rector of Starston, and Mary Friston, widow, of y⁰ same parish, were married y⁰ 30th day of May, Ann. 1704.

1712. William, y⁰ son of Alice Pwsw [I cannot decipher this name], a servant of Mr. Sancroft of Fresonfield in Suffolk, being drown'd on y⁰ 25, at Framingham in Suffolk, was here buried on y⁰ 29 day of Nov., 1712 (fee, 6/8).

1729. Mr. Thomas Arrowsmith, late rector, was buried March y⁰ 31, 1729.

1734. March 6, was buried Samuel Mills, who had been clerk of this parish upwards of 30 years. No one was ever known to speak ill of him, and he is said to have had not one enemy in the world : a rare instance of Felicity. This testimony, I thought, was due to the memory of so innocent and pious a man.

Fairfax Stillingfleet, M.A.,
Curate.

1741. Philip Williams, D.D., rector of this parish, was married May 26th, 1741, to Ann Dighton, daughter of John Dighton, D.D., rector of Newmarket, and Elizabeth his wife, in Jesus College Chappell, Cambridge, by Ch. Ashton, D.D., Master of the said College.

John Baron, half Brother of the late Dean of Norwich, buried Jan. 5.

1742. A Baptism by Rev. Gervas Holmes, vicar of Fressingfield.

A COPY OF A PARISH ORDER.

Agreed at a parish meeting this second day of December, 1742, that the thanks of the ministers, churchwardens, and inhabitants of ye parish of Starston be given to Mrs. Sancroft, for her late handsome present of plate to the said parish church, consisting of one silver chalice and cover, and of one silver paten, and that Dr. Williams be deputed to wait on ye said lady, and in ye name of ye parish to present the same to her.

Ph. Williams,
Rector of ye parish.

N.B.—The above communion plate was ye private communion plate of ye late Archbishop Sancroft, after his deprivation in his chappel at Freshingfield ; ye inscription upon the side of ye cup and upon ye rim of ye patin—

DEO
SERVATORI
SACRUM.

Upon ye top of ye cover—1567. The weight of all, above twenty ounces.

The lady who gave it—Catherine, widow of Wm. Sancroft, Esq., and fourth daughter of Sir John Cotton, Baronet.

A parish order in ye same form was made Dec. 27, 1742, to return to Miss Catherine Sancroft, 2^d daughter of ye before-named Wm. and Catherine Sancroft, ye thanks of the minister, churchwardens, and inhabitants for a present made by her to the communion table of one fine Damask Table Cloath, and of one Damask Napkin, on wh^ch is woven ye story of ye good Samaritan pouring oil and wine into y^o traveller's wounds. It is marked—W. S. ; and ye Table Cloath is a forest piece, and marked—W. C.

Cash contributed by ye following persons towards a new pulpit :—

	£.	s.	d.
Waldgrave Pelham, Esq. . .	2	2	0
T. Tenison, LL.D.	2	2	0
Ph. Williams, D.D.	1	1	0

BRIEFS COLLECTED AT STARSTON, 1745 :—

St. Alban's, loss by Fire, £1384,

     read Dec. 2, 1745 . . 3s. 6d.

Hythe Church, Kent, £1100,

    read and collected August 24th . . 2s.

[There are eleven such briefs recorded.]

N.B.—The dial on yᵉ south side of yᵉ tower was put up at yᵉ expense of £2. 15s. 0d. by Ph. Wms.

MEM., Dec. 25, 1737.

The Velvet Pulpit Cushion was given by Philip Williams, Rector. The cussion was yᵉ Right Honᵇˡᵉ yᵉ Lord Blaney's of Ireland, of St. John's College in Cambridge, wᶜʰ used to be laid in yᵉ University Church for his Lordship's use upon Sundays and Holidays, and was given to me by his Tutor, H. Wrigley, B.D. The gold and silk tassels were purchased by me at £1. 15s. 0d. The stuff of yᵉ case was given by my Draper, J. Mortlock, and yᵉ making of it by J. Willson, my Taylor, and the wainscoat box, in wᶜʰ it came, by Joh. Smith, my Joyner.

          Ph. Wms.

[MEM.—I can find no trace of either Miss Sancroft's work, or the above cushion, which we may assume has long been worn out.

There are no registers of much interest since then.]

THE STARSTON TOWNE BOOKE.

This book is still in a fair state of preservation, and its interest lies in the light which it throws on English history in villages during the Commonwealth, and the stormy times before and after. The writing on most pages is excellent; in almost all cases easily legible after a little practice. It will be seen to be the immediate precursor of the present churchwardens' book.

The magistrates who countersigned the accounts were, among others, Sir Thomas Gawdy and Tobias Frere. Sir T. Gawdy was the owner of Gawdy Hall, and, as a Royalist, mortgaged his property to Toby Frere, in order to raise money for the king. He never regained it, and from Mr. Frere it almost immediately passed to Mr. Wogan, of whom a descendant, John Wogan, married Elizabeth Sancroft, the heiress of the Archbishop.

Toby Frere is, I believe, an ancestor of the family of Freres at Roydon. He lived at Caltofts, Harleston (Mr. Hazard's house.) He is buried at Redenhall; and his monument is on the west end of the church, nearly hidden by the gallery.

STARSTON TOWNE BOOK,

Beginning April, 1622; ending April 7th, 1670:—

| Starston, Anno Dni. 1622. | The accompts of Thomas ffuller, Churchwarden of Starston, aforesaid, |

and Robt. fflatman and Thomas Groome, overfseers
of the poore for the yeare just past, ended at our
Lady, 1623.

Imprimis, Received of Mr. Cotton   Outdwellers.
         „   of Mr. Tayburgh of the Lady Gawdy.

1623. The accompts of the churchwardens and overfseers
       for the poore of the Towneship of Starston for
       poore money by them received and howe dis-
       tributed towards the reliefe of the poore for one
       whole yeare, 1623 until 1624, as followeth :—
Imprimis, Received for the whole yeare,   Outdwellers.
       of Mr. Cotton, xxvij*s*.   of the Lady Gawdy, v*s*.
          Sum total, £viij. xix*s*. viij*d*.

1624. [Not in the book.]

1625. The accompts of the two Churchwardens for one
       yeare, beginning at Easter, 1625, untill Easter,
       1626.

Disbursem̃ts.

Item for fencing the Towne house yard, 1*s*. 1*d*.
Item more laid out to Willm. Hills that his rate no fall
       short.
Item more layed out for a Book for the Towne.
Item of Mr. Cotton for one year's rent of the Towne poor
       in Barnsfield ended at our Lady, 1626, 10*s*. viij*d*.

1626. ⎞
1627. ⎪
      ⎬ [Not in the book.]
1628. ⎪
1629. ⎠

Starston,   The Accompts of Thomas ffuller and Tho.
  1630.   Humphrey, overfseers for ye poore of Starston
        aforesaid, made for one whole year ending in y^e
        yeare 1631.

Receypts.   Outdwellers.
Imprimis, Mr. Cotton, 12s. 6d.   Thomas Gawdy, Kt., 5s.

Disbursemts.
To blind Ann, 3s.

1632. The accompts of John ffuller and John Baker,
        overfseers for the poore, for one whole yeare
        ended at Easter last, as followeth :—
Imprimis, Barth. Cotton, Esq., 10s.   Outdwellers.
                                  Tho. Gawdy, Kt., 3s. 4d.
                                  Mr. Gleane, 10s.

Disbursemts.
To blind Ann, iijs.
To ye widd. Gissing, xvijs. iijd.

1633. [Nothing of particular interest.]

1634.   „   „   „

1635. The accompts of William Linton, gent, and . .
        . . . . overfseers for the poore of the Towne
        of Starston for one whole year, beginning a week
        before Easter last, 1634, and ending this Easter,
        1635.
                    Disbursements.
It. for enteringe into booke this our accompt, 8d.

1636. ⎫
1637. ⎭ [Nothing of much interest.]

1638. ⎫
1639. ⎭ [Not in the book.]

Sterstone, the 6th day   The accompt of Richard Ward
of April, Ano. 1640.   and Bartholomew Lenold, overfseers
for the poore of yᵉ said towne
for yᵉ yeare now ended, in yᵉ time of William
Bartroope and Thomas Kidman, churchwardens,
wherein the receipts and also the payments for
yᵉ whole year as followeth:—

		£.	s.	d.	
Imprimis, of Mr. Lyndall, gent.		oi	o2	6	Outdwellers.
of Mr. Anguish Clarke		oo	o7	i	of Thomas
of Mr. Lynton . . .		oo	i4	i	Gleane, Esq.
of Daniell Richards .		oo	ii	6	

1641. The accompt of Thomas ffuller—

Imprimis of John Tyndall, Gent. . .   . xxiv*s*. iij*d*.
of Mr. Anguish, Rector . . . .   xiij*s*. iiij*d*.

1642. The accompts of Laurence Maihew
and Thomas ffuller—

Receipts.
Imprimis, Richard Anguish, Rector . . . . . 10*s*. 4*d*.

1643. The accompt of Daniell Richards—

Receipts.
Imprimis, Richard Anguish, Rector . . .   . 7*s*. 9*d*.

Starston, the 22th of   The accompt of John ffuller and
aprill, Anno dom. 1644.   John Baker, overfseers for the
poore of the said Towne, for
the yeare nowe ended in the tyme of John Wyth,

gent., and John Richards, churchwardens, wherein the receipts and alſo the payments for the whole yeare are expreſed and sett downe as followeth:—

Receipts.

	£.	s.	d.
Imprimis, Richard Anguish, Rector	o	6	i
John Tasborough, gent.	o	i	o
William Linton, gent.	o	iij	o
John Linton, gent.	o	i	o
John Wyth, gent.	i	ii	i
Joell Trundell, gent.	o	ii	o
Daniel Richards	i	iiij	i

Outt dwellers.

	£.	s.	d.
Thomas Gleane, Esq.	o	iij	j
Richard Taylor, gent.	o	i	i
John Taylor, gent.	o	ii	o

Disbursemᵗˢ.

	£.	s.	d.
It'm for a payer of shoues for the bigest boy . .	o	i	4
It'm for 3 yards 3 quarters of saking to make his clothis	o	2	4
It'm pay'd to bartholomew seabold for making them, and for lyneings he put on . . .	o	3	o
It'm for tooe yards and a halfe of clothe to make him to shirts	o	i	io
It'm to the widd. Alger for making his shirts .	o	o	5
It'm for a payer of hose for him	o	i	o
It'm for a payer of shoues and a weskote for the moother	o	o	io
It'm for fuston to make the youngest gurle tooe bloyses	o	o	6

$£.$ $s.$ $d.$

It'm for lining clothe to make the youngest boy
    a shirt . . . . o   i   o
    We allow this account till cause be shown
    to the contrarie.

                  John Smythe.   Dr. Corie.

Starston,   The accompts of John Tasburgh and
14th of aprill, Edward Ollef, overſeers for the poore of
    1645.   the said towne, for the yeare now ended
                 in the tyme of Will. Linton and Daniell
        Richards, churchwardens, wherein the receipts and
        alſoe the payem[ts] for the whole yeare are ex-
        pressed and sett down as followeth:—

Imprimis, the sequestrators for   Outdwellers,
    the gleb lands and other {   Thomas Gleane,
    benefettes that ariss to } $£o. 10s.$ Esq.
    the Church   }

                                    $£.$ $s.$ $d.$

John Tasborough . .   . .   o   4   o
Will. Linton, gent. .   .   .   o   7 10
John With, gent.   o 15   4
Daniell Richards   i   2   2
Lar. Mayhew   .   .   . . o   7   9

    Seene and allowed, 14 Aprill, 1645, untill cause be
    proved to y[e] contrary,
                         Tho. Gawdy,
                         To. ffrere.

1646.   [Nothing of particular interest.]

Starston, 20th of   The Accompt of Abraham Aldys and
    Aprill, 1647.   Edward Tibenham, overſeers for the
                     pore of the said Towne for the yeare
            now ended in the time of Robert Jermyn and

John Levould, churchwardens, wherein what they have received and also what they have laid out in the whole yeare is set downe as followeth :—

Receipts.

	£.	s.	d.
Imprimis, received of John Tasborough . .	0	3	9
„ William Linton, gent. . .	0	2	0
„ Mr. Kent, cler.	0	1	0
„ Mrs Anne Haies, wid. . .	0	1	0

Outdwellers.

Thomas Glene, Esq.	0	2	4
Richard Sayer, gent.	0	1	0
Elizabeth Mayhew	0	0	3
Widdow Etheridge	0	0	4

The Difburfements.

paid for two pairs of Endentures for two pore children	0	4	0
given to Richard Baker in the time of his wive's fickness	0	2	0
given to the Clark for writing a Certificate . .	0	0	6
laid out for my dynner and for my horfse at Stratton	0	1	2

We allow of this account till cause be shown to the contrary,
John Smythe. To. ffrere.

1648. The Accompts of Robbt. Todd—

Imprimis, received of Robbt. Kent, Clarke . .	0	2	0

Difburfments.

laid ought more for his washing and fireing . .	1	5	0
laid ought more for a shurt for him . . .	0	3	4

£. s. d.

payd to William ffuller for making the Wid.
. . . . grave . . . . o i o
paid to Zacary Woodding for a payer of shoues
      for him . . . . o 2 4
laid ought more for a shurt for him, and for
      saking for a cote for him, and for
      making of them . . . . o 7 5
laid more for a payer of briches for him . . . o 3 4
laid ought to goodwyfe Baker for washing of
      Zacary Woodding . . . . o 6 o

1649.) [Nothing of much interest is recorded.
1650.) Robert Kent, Clarke.]

1651. The accompts of Edward ffuller—

                          s. d.   s. d.

Imprimis, Robert Kent, Clarke 10 o Thomas Gleane 2 4
        Luckin Cotton, gent. 5 10

Difbursments.

Payd to Zacary Moude in the time of his nede   5 o

1652. The accompts of Robert Game—

Imprimis, Luckin Cotton, gent. 14 7
        Robert Kent, Clarke 11 3

Difburfements.

layd out to the widd. Clark for washinge Andry
      Martin . . . . 10 o

1653. The accompt of Tho. Wales—

Imprimis, Luckin Cotton, gent. . . . . . o 12 6
       Mr. Robt. Kent, Minister . . . . . o 5 o
now Mr. Thomas ffifher, minister . . . . o 5 o

1654. The accompt of Robt. fering, gent.—

	£.	s.	d.
Imprimis, Luckin Cotton, gent.	o	13	4
Mr. Thomas ffifher, minister	o	10	o

1655. The accompts of John Barthroppe—

Imprimis, Mr. Cotton, gent.	o	15	3
Mr. Thomas ffisher, Clarke . . .	o	11	3

1656. The Accompt of William Reade—

Imprimis, Mr. ffisher, clarke	o	5	o
Mr. Cotton	o	6	8

Difbursements.

given to other poore people in the time of thear sickness	o	2	o
layd out for thear wood for the winter	o	6	8
layed out for fower shifts and making of them for Mooer's children	o	6	8

1657. The accompts of Danyell Andrewes—

Imprimis, Mr. Tho. ffisher	o	7	o
Mr. Cotton	o	9	o

1658. [Nothing of interest.]

1659. [Nothing of interest.]

1660. [Not in the book.]

1661. The accompts of John Wythe—

Imprimis, Mr. Smalpeece	1	1	8
Mr. ffifher and Mr. Spendlove . . .	o	12	6

[At the accession, Fisher seems to have been ejected in favour of Spendlove.]

1662.   The accompts of John ffuller—

	£.	s.	d.	
Imprimis, Mr. Smalpeece	0	12	0	Outdwellers.
Mr. Spendlove	0	10	0	Petter Gleane, Esq.
				£1. 2s. 6d.

1663 to 1668.   [Nothing of interest.   No reference to any
      clergyman during this time.]

1669.   The account of ffrances Richards—
for carrying three lods of wood to the towne house, £0. 4s. 0d.

1670.   The Accompt of Laurence Maihew—
Rich. Luthwhite, £0. 2s. 4d.   Outdwellers.
                                 Mr. Wogon, £0. 2s. 7d.

Aprill 7th, 1670.

Wee allow this accompt till good cause
be showed to the contrary,

Peter Gleane,
Robt. Kemp.

CHURCHWARDENS OF STARSTON.

1686.	Daniell Creake.	James Seamon.
1687.	John Carter.	Samuel Tubby.
1688.	Francis Buxton.	Wm. Mingay.
1690.	Francis Buxton.	William Vines.

1692.	Francis Buxton.	Samuel Tubby.
1693.	William Richards.	Henry Adkins.
1694.	William Mingay.	Samuel Tubby.
1695.	„ „	Robert Chittocks.
1696.	John Neech.	„ „
1697.	Edw. Jubee.	Edw. ffuller.
1698.	Edw. Juby.	John Barber.
1699.	Simon Wainford.	John Baker.
1700.	„ „	Tasburgh Lewse.
1701.	Francis Buxton.	James Meen.
1702.	William Mingay.	Thomas Corbold.
1703.	„ „	Thomas Flatman.
1704.	William Smith.	Thomas Folkard.
1705.	Robert Chittock.	Thomas Evans.
1706.	Francis Buxton, *gent.*	Thomas Flatman.
1707.	Daniel Creake.	Simon Wainforth.
1708.	„ „	Tasburgh Rewse.
1709.	Francis Buxton.	„ „
1710.	„ „	Wood Savage.
1711.	Tasburgh Rewse.	Daniel Creake.
1712.	Joshua Meen.	„ „
1713.	John Seaman.	„ „
1714.	William Mendham.	James Barber.
1715.	„ „	Thomas Dallison.
1716.	„ „	Lach Gower.
1717.	Tasburgh Rewse.	Daniel Creake.
1718.	Simon Wainforth.	„ „
1719-20.	„ „	„ „
1721.	John Swan.	James Barber.
1722.	Robert Fuller.	„ „
1723.	Thomas Manning.	Daniel Creake.
1724.	„ „	„ „
1725.	„ „	„ „
1726.	„ „	Richard Page.

1729.	Thomas Manning.	[only one apparently, this year.]
1730.	Daniel Creake.	Richard Page.
1731.	Thomas Manning.	Thomas Corbould.
1732.	,,　　　　,,	John Tuthill.
1735.	,,　　　　,,	John Moor.
1736-37.	,,　　　　,,	James Fuller.
1738.	,,　　　　,,	Thomas Evans.
1739.	,,　　　　,,	Daniel Creake.
1742.	,,　　　　,,	John Moore.
1749.	John Tuthill.	,,　　　　,,
1751.	,,　　　　,,	Robert Bond.
1752.	,,　　　　,,	John Moore.
1753.	,,　　　　,,	Robert Bond.
1755.	,,　　　　,,	John Gooding.
1757.	,,　　　　,,	Robert Kemp.
1760.	,,　　　　,,	Thomas Walne.
1761.	,,　　　　,,	John Gooding.
1762.	,,　　　　,,	Robert Kemp.
1763.	,,　　　　,,	Buxton Moore.
1766.	,,　　　　,,	Robert Kemp.
1767.	,,　　　　,,	Buxton Moore, (till)
1781.	,,　　　　,,	Robert Kemp.
1782.	,,　　　　,,	George Theobald.
1783.	William Fisk.	,,　　　　,,
1788.	,,　　　　,,	John Porter.
1790.	George Fisk.	John Howlett.
1791.	,,　　　　,,	John Porter.
1792.	,,　.　　,,	John Walne.
1794.	,,　　　　,,	William Cole.
1807.	Thomas Lingwood.	William Cole.
1808.	,,　　　　,,	John Theobald.
1825.	C. Etheridge.	J. Theobald.
1843.	,,　　　　,,	David Feaveryer.

1861.	C. Etheridge.	Benjamin Burgess.
1868.	J. E. Lacon.	„ „
1871.	„ „	Thomas Mullenger.
1874.	J. R. Palmer.	,, ,,
1879.	D. I. Danby.	Alfred Taylor.

CHURCHWARDENS' BOOK.

[P. 3.] Rev. W. Whitear read the 39 Articles 20 Novr 1803. Died December 10, 1826, from a gunshot wound inflicted by Thomas Pallant on the night of the 27 November, who, being out watching in company with the above and others, fired at him thro' mistake, being at the same time much alarmed. Buried 16 Dec^r, 1826.

[Next page.] The Rev. Wm. Pakenham Spencer, Rector, presented the church with an organ, which was opened on Easter Sunday, in the year 1838.

		£.	s.	d.
1699.	Collected in Starston for the ffrench Prostatant [*i.e.*, Protestant] ...... the 5,			
	1699. The amount is		10	1
	This Churchwardens' Book was bought in 1686.			
1686.	It. laid out at the parambilation . . .		15	0
	It. to six travellers		1	0
	[And many more such.]			
	For wood for the gleasors (glaziers) to heat their irons			2
	Clark's wages	1	4	0

E

	£.	s.	d.
1686. For scouring the flagons		1	0
1687. ffor washing the surplice		2	0
ffor 12 seamen		1	0
1688. Pd. Goody Greak for washing the surplice		2	0
Pd. Creak for an order to pray for P. W.			6
[James II. had abdicated ; William III. then ascended the throne.]			
An order for praying for K. W. and Q. M.			6
1689. Spent at yᵉ coronation of King Willᵐ and Queen Mary		6	0
Layd out for a fox killing		1	0
Given towards a burning to two men .		1	0
Given to a poor man burnt by lightning and thunder			6
1690. Pd. to a petition for a burning to Hinghā			
An order frō Sʳ Peter* to remove old king [i.e., the king's name from the Liturgy]		2	0
Given to yᵉ ringers at king William's return		2	6
Expended at Hardwick vⁿ to remove old king		1	8
Given a poor man undone by fire . . .			9
1692. A man burnt by thunder and lightning .			6
[And so several times again.]			
1694. for yᵉ surplis, and for towlling yᵉ bell for ye queen Mar. 5, 1694.			
1696. For ye clapper of ye bell	10	0	

---

* Sir Peter Gleane, Baronet, of Hardwick, was the local magnate in those days. He is buried within Hardwick Church; and the present vestry there was the old gentleman's private pew.

		£.	s.	d.
1697.	Given to ye ringers at powder Plot . .		2	6
1698.	Given to yᵉ passengers undone by water floods			7
1700.	Given to two that lost their ship coming from the Indies			2
	Jan. 27. Disbursed to old Gower by general consent		2	6
1706.	Given to ye ringers at Coronation day .		1	6
1708.	Given to one John Amos, with a petition for a loss of 100 and 18 lbs. and upwards of his cattle dyeing of yᵉ murraygne, who came from Huddingham in yᵉ isle of Ely		1	0
1709.	Paid to ye visitors that came to view the church [? Archdeacon's visitation] .		2	10
	Given to a sick soldier passing to his home in Kent			2
1711.	Paid to Mr. Page for painting the Queen's arms and the commandments . .	2	0	0
1712.	I gave to six passengers			3
1721.	I paid to Thomas Seaman for hanging the five bells, and for timber and for small irons	12	0	0
	Paid to him more for making a new wheel for the fourth bell and hanging of it .		15	0
	Laid out to ye Blacksmith for a clapper, & mending one of ye Bells		5	4
	Spent in putting yᵉ Bells to yᵉ Repayring		1	6
	Spent at yᵉ ffinishing of yᵉ Bells . .		2	6
	for wine at yᵉ Communion at Michᵐˢ .		4	6

[Until now, apparently only three times a year.]

| 1723, Feb. 26. | Going to Norwich to put ye Bell out . . . . | | 5 | 8 |
| | The Bell ffounder's bill . . . . . . | 10 | 12 | 6 |

	£.	s.	d.

1728, May 30. Laid out in going ye bounds . 1 7 6

1731. For removing Goody Masting to yᵉ
    Towne House 4 0

1734. Paid postage of a letter sent by Borret
    from Greenwich (?)   4

1735, July 30. For brade and wine 1 10
    October 4.   „   „ 1 10

1739. to Brade and wine at Wisentide . . .   2 1
    August yᵉ 4th. Brade and wine . . .   1 10
    September ye 20.   „   . . .   1 10

1740. To Brad and wine at Christmas . . .   3 00
    to Brad and wine the Sunday after
    Christmas Day 1 11

1742. [Bread and wine accounts every month.]

1743. [Ditto till 1772. George Davies died
    1768.]

1744. Paid for sparrows 1 9 8

1746. Pd. more for 137 dozen sparrows, 3d. a
    dozen 1 14 3

1747. Pd. to ye Carpenter for mending the
    grate Bell 1 4 0

1772. Paid for a Clause of Mr. Davis' will . .   2 6

1774. A Hood for Dr. Frampton 2 2 6

1777. Bread and wine for several sacraments .   4 0

1784. Pd. the Rev. Mr. Malom 13 0

1786. Pd. for 83 dozen and 7 sparrows . . . 1 0 10¾

1787. Pd. for a letter from Cambridge . .   4

1794. Gave the ringers by desire of Mr.
    Etheridge on the king's birthday .   5 0
    Pd. for Sparrows, pr. Acct. 227½ dozen 2 16 10½

1795. Gave Aldburgh singers 2 6

1797. Paid for a letter respecting the hair
    powder   6

Inhabitants numbered May 1, 1798 :—

96 men

125 women

82 girls under 15 years of age

82 boys under do.

385 Total in 1798

215 in 1698

170 Increase of inhabitants in a century.

		£.	s.	d.
1799.	Tho⁸ Aggas, Clerk's salary	2	2	0

[Hitherto always £1. 4s.]

1801. Names of persons who went the bounds
of the parish 16 May, 1801 :—

Farmers.

Thos. Lingwood   Sam¹ Chambers

Geo. Fisk   Wm. Cole

Thos. Walne   John Theobald

John Coleby

Labourers and others, 18.

[Among them Jonas Ellis.]

It cost	2	4	6

1803. Prayer for his Majesty after the ex-
ecution of Despard, &c., &c., for high
treason 1 0

1806. John Brown attending Children at
Church 5 0

1807. [Holy communion only four times a
year.]

1808. John Burgess for repairing the bells, as
per bill 18 19 0

[No notice of payment to ringers since
1794.]

1811. A new Surplice 3 3 0

	£.	s.	d.

1814.   Starston is 10¾ miles round it.

1819, Aug. 3.   Paid for 104 dozen sparrows at
 3*d*. . . . . | 1 | 6 | 0 |

March 20.   56¾ dozen old ones at 6*d*.   . | 1 | 8 | 4 |

„   For new Oak Altar Piece, as
per bill [*i.e.*, a reredos for
the Commandments, Lord's
Prayer, and Creed] . . . | 20 | 16 | 6 |

1819, Ap. 2.   Apparitor buying of papers from
association for Propagating religion in
foreing Parts . . . . | | 1 | 0 |

T. Agas, tolling the bell 6 hours upon
death of king . . . . | | 7 | 6 |

1822.   Apparitor, for bringing letters for sub-
scription for Irish poor . . . . . | | 1 | 0 |

1823.   Goldspink, for 18 hassocks for Church,
2*s*. 6*d*. each . . . . | 2 | 5 | 3 |

Do., 25 feet of mat for laying against
the rails that surround the Communion
table, at 3*d*. per foot . . . . . . | | 6 | 3 |

1827.   Knights, tolling the bell 4 hours at Duke
of York's funeral . . . . | | 4 | 0 |

1828.   Mrs. Jackson, ¼ salary for Sunday
school . . . . | | 18 | 0 |

[Regularly thereafter.]

[Full account of workhouse built. It cost
£238. 10*s*.; contract, £420 in all. Full
details are given, covering four pages.]

1830.   Tolling bell 6 hours at death of king
George the 4th . . . . | | 7 | 6 |

1831, Sept. 4.   Given ringers at Coronation of
William the fourth . . . . | | 10 | 0 |

1838.   Tolling the bell at the death of king
William the 4th, 3 hours . . . . . | | 3 | 0 |

£. s. d.

1839. [Sundry expenses for the school, built this year.]

1840. Pd. for ringing the bells at the Queen's wedding 10 0

1840, June 19. Postage of form of prayer and thanksgiving, Queen's escape from assassination   5

1842, Feb. 15. Order for the Prince Albert Edw. of Wales being inserted in Liturgy   6

For ringers when he was born 10 0

1845. The porch of the church was repaired; the front being rebuilt at the Parish expense in August, 1845.

1848. Pd. Hart for tuning the Organ . . . 1 15

Rev. G. B. Kingdon, donation for the Niche in the porch 3 0 0

1855, 22 Nov. John Bunn appointed clerk in room of Isaac Kent, deceased.

[No items of great interest since then.]

In old days, when the tithes were paid in kind, the immense labour caused thereby was often settled by a compromise. I have several note books filled in by Mr. Wyat, Mr. Arrowsmith, and other rectors, besides deeds in the handwriting of Ric. Anguish and Cuthbert Browne.

The following are a few specimens :—

MR. WIAT'S BOOK No. 1.

	£.	s.
Mr. Wogan, for all tiths	2	5
Mr. Carter, ffor all tithes for seven years, per annum	5	15

A fat goose, a fat turkey, 2 dozen and a halfe
of pigeons.

MR. ARROWSMITH'S BOOK, No. 3.

All sorts of wood in yᵉ parish of Starston is tythable, provided they make fuell of it.

Memd. on yᵉ 15 day of May, 1722, Mr. Manning yᵉ younger brother Simon Wainforth's exd-cute (*sic*) expressd great wrath agt me, for refusing to suffer his uncle to be buried in yᵉ church, who was a person yᵗ had lived in contempt of all ministeriall ordinances, in wrath and defiance to me his lawfull minister had left his church for upwards of 13 years, and had admitted himself into the sect of the Quakers, and yet his relations desired that he might lie in yᵉ Church and have Xtian buryall, wch I refusᵈ, and so he was carryed to Raydon.

		s.	d.
1727.	Allowed him for a double barrel of oysters	7	0
1721.	Then received of dried hops which I took for tithe off Dr. Tennison's farm where Henry Richards dwelleth .	*57 pounds.*	
1726.	I have had of goodman Bun 24 loads of muck at eight pence a load, comes to	*16 sh.*	
April 7th, 1717.	Then recᵈ of Danl Creak for his two closes and his hemp land, for two years	0 14	0
At yᵉ same time payd him for a wig	10	1

		£.	s.	d.
April 2, 1719.	For 2 firkins of butter	2	8	0
	For yᵉ taxes	1	19	9
	For yᵉ window tax	0	15	0
	And in money	3	17	3
Jan. 26	Receiv'd for a corps at Alburgh . . .	0	5	0
	Receiv'd for a marriage	0	5	0

THE SCHOOL.

In old days schools were indeed few and far between. Larger towns had their Grammar School, but country villages were dependent on certain old ladies—dames, as they were called—who used to teach what they could. Mrs. Kent, our patriarch, now ninety-five years old, widow of Isaac Kent the clerk, tells me that when she was young, girls were taught to knit, but were seldom taught their letters.

Mrs. Jackson, who was paid every quarter from 1828 for teaching the Sunday school, was, I suppose, our first mistress.

The present school was built in 1839 by Mr. Spencer, who certainly started most of the educational work in the village. The class-room was built in 1855 (£30), and enlarged in 1877 (£53), at the sole charge of Archdeacon Hopper.

There are, this year, nearly a hundred children on the books, and the attendance is often over ninety— so great is the thirst for education in these days.

STARSTON PARISH CHARITIES.

There is nothing of any great interest about the charities of this parish. In the year 1865 various old charities were, with the consent of the Charity Commissioners, consolidated, and two fields lying west of the road to Hardwick were bought with the proceeds. The trustees are the Rector, Church-wardens, and Overseers—all ex-officio; and the proceeds are divided among the poor shortly before Christmas.

The Titlow Trust. Rev. Samuel Titlow, a poor boy of Harleston, was first helped with his education by Rev. W. Whitear, Rector of Starston. At his death in 1872 he left the sum of £800, the proceeds of which are used, five years out of six, in apprenticing poor boys from the above parishes, Redenhall having four turns to one for Starston. In the sixth year, after any necessary repairs to the testator's grave, the surplus is handed over to the rectors of the two parishes, in the same proportion.

———

After the facts given I have little more left to say; but two things seem to have always worked together for the prosperity of Starston: one, the fact

of there being a good rectory house, at which there
has almost always been a resident rector, who, from
the peculiar facts of the patronage, would be always a
distinguished man ; secondly, that there has always
been a good house and tenant at Starston Place.
While many other parishes were served by curates,
with perhaps one service a fortnight, the rector
living possibly on the other side of the country, all
the rectors of Starston lived among their people, as
is proved by their tithe books and the registers.

I have noted that when George Davies became
rector, the Holy Communion was administered every
month, or even oftener, while three or four times a
year had been the rule before.

Dr. Frampton, at first resident, was the sole
exception. For the last fourteen years he was non-
resident, living at Newmarket for the sake of
racing. The last of the curates-in-charge was the
Rev. Robert Etheredge, father of our late respected
churchwarden, who died in 1867.

Mr. Whitear was a most active man in the parish
and in the neighbourhood, as a magistrate. During
his incumbency the battle of Waterloo was fought ;
and during the great excitement just previous, I have
been told that arrangements had quite been made
to take all the women and children to Rushall : Mr.
Whitear and Archdeacon Oldershaw were to lead
the Starston men to any work such a troublous time

as war, and soldiers over-running the country, might need.

Protection of life and property, resistance to cruelty and pillage, might easily have needed strong action and courage, both of which were found ready in Mr. Whitear. Happily, the victory of Waterloo made all such preparations unnecessary.

His death has already been described in an extract from the churchwardens' book. Mr. Whitear had consented, as a magistrate, to go with a party of farmers and others in search of a gang of poachers, who were said to infest the Gawdy Hall woods. With them went one Thomas Pallant, a young man, the nephew of the occupier of Starston Hall. All were armed with guns, and by some mistake, in the darkness of the night, young Pallant fired at Mr. Whitear, who, in his turn, fired at Pallant. Mr. Whitear was mortally wounded, and died in thirteen days, from the effects. There is a monument to his memory over the vestry door, the inscription being written by the Rev. John Oldershaw, Rector of Redenhall and Archdeacon of Norfolk.

The good work begun by Mr. Whitear was continued by Mr. Spencer, and especially by Archdeacon Hopper, of which accounts will be found under the head of the church, the school, &c. Archdeacon Hopper was one of the earliest school examiners in the diocese; and after being Honorary Canon and Proctor in Convocation, was appointed Archdeacon of Norwich in 1868.

No rector of Starston has come here with such distinguished university honours as Mr. Watson. He was twelfth wrangler, first class in the theological tripos, also Tyrwhitt and Crosse scholar ; and while Rector of Starston he preached a course of Hulsean lectures before the University.

After being eight years Rector of Starston he accepted an offer made to him, to return to his old work at the University.

On his resignation, all the Fellows of S. John's College in orders declined the living, which was accepted by the present rector, on his own nomination.

Of the three following deeds, now among the rector's papers, the first is an agreement between Richard Anguish and the sequestrators of the living, in 1646 ; the second, a deed by which Cuthbert Browne, for a consideration, obtained this living ; and the third, by Philip Williams, is interesting with reference to the rectory and the state of farming in his times :—

I.

xiv. ffebruary, 1646.

Knowe all men by these presents that I, Richard Anguishe, late of Starston in the county of Norff., then have per cha'd of John Wythe, gent., William Lynton, gent., Daniell Richards, and Laurence Mayhew, sequestrators of the livinge of Starston aforesaid the some of eighteen pounds nineteen shillings and four pence, ordered and delivered by the Land mortgage comittee for this countie to be paid to me by the said sequestrators as by the said order dated the xiv. ffebruary, 1646, appeareth ffor the arrears of the effects of the said livinge of Starston untill Mr. Kent do take uppon him the care of the said livinge. And the said Richard Anguishe, if he do thereby agree that if he the said Richard shall hereafter recover to his ward (?) that or his wyfe (?) the fifth parte of the effects of the said livinge by vertue of any indenture of . . . . . heretofore made. That thereupon it shall be lawfull for the said sequestrators, or any other enjoying the said livinge to deduct or defaulte from the said Richard the said some of xviii£. xixs. vid. out of the said fifty £., and that this his hand shall be sufficient discharge therefore, for witness whereof the said Richard Anguishe gave hereunto all his hand and seale the day and yeare above said.

Sealed and delivered in the
p'sence of

| Ric. Rayeth, | Vexa Cogia, |
| John Smith. | Ric. Anguish. |

II.

To whom these presents shall come, The Right Hono^ble Henry Lord Mowbray, comonly called Earle of Arundell, son and heir apparent of Henry Duke of Norfolk, The Right Hono^ble Francis Lord Howard of Effingham, Paul Rycant of the parish of St. Martin in the feilds in the County of Middx., Esq., and Cuthbert Browne of Hansworth in the County of York, Clerke, send Greeting.   Whereas the said

Henry Lord Mowbray, Francis Lord Howard, Paul Rycant, and Cuthbert Browne, some or one of them at the time of the sealing and delivery hereof are or is instituted unto the Advowson Donation Collation presentation and free disposition of the parish church of Starston als. Sterston in the County of Norfolk. Now know yee that they the said Henry Lord Mowbray, Francis Lord Howard, Paul Rycant, and Cuthbert Browne, for divers good causes and considerations them thereunto especially moveing, Have given granted and Assigned, and by these presents doe give grant and Assigne unto John Burbury of Albury in the County of Surrey, gent., his Executors and Assignes the next Advowson Donation Collation presentation and free disposition of the parish Church aforesaid for the next avoydance and next Advowson only, so that it shall be lawful for the said John Burbury his Executors and Assignes, any fit person to the said Church to the Diocesan of the same, or any other Competent Judge in that behalfe, to present when the said Church by death resignation privation cession or by any other means shall happen to be voyd. In witnesse whereof the said Henry Lord Mowbray, Francis Lord Howard, Paul Rycant, and Cuthbert Browne, have hereunto sett their hands and sealed this Thirtieth day of May In the yeare of Lord, 1682.

Arundell,
Effingham,
Paul Rycant,
Cuthbert Browne.

III.

Memorandum. Sept. 29, 1732. It is covenanted and agreed between Philip Williams, D.D., Rector of Starston, on ye one hand, and Richard Britin, Husbandman, of ye same place on ye other in matter and form following, viz., y^t ye said Richd Britin shall possess and occupy according to ye rules of husbandry all those Glebe Lands of ye aforesaid Rectory, and all those Lands wch were held in lieu of Glebe, and were lately in ye occupation of ye late Rev^d Mr. Thomas Arrowsmith, and since of his sister, Mrs. Margaret Arrowsmith ; together wth the Parsonage House, outhouses, Gardens, orchards, and all the appurtenances thereunto belonging : and ye said Philip Williams doth, by these presents, demise, grant, and to farm let to ye said Richard Britin, his heirs, Ex^{rs}, and Adm^{rs}, ye above-named Parsonage House and out Houses, Glebe Lands, and Lands in lieu of Glebe ; To have and to hold the same, free from ye payment of all matter of Tyths for ye full term of three years, commencing from ye day of ye date hereof, and ending on ye feast of St. Michael in ye year of our Lord, 1735 ; provided y^t ye above-named Philip Williams so long continues Rector of Starston : and ye above-named Richard Britin, his heirs, Ex^{rs}, and Adm^{rs}, yeilding and paying therefore to ye aforesaid Philip Williams, his heirs, Ex^{rs}, and Adm^{rs}, ye sum of thirty-five pounds yearly at two equal payments, viz., seventeen pounds and ten shillings upon Lady Day next ensuing, and seventeen pounds and ten shillings upon Michaelmas Day following, and go on for ye whole term of three years, expressed in this agreement, provided likewise y^t ye said Richard Britin, his heirs, Ex^{rs}, and Adm^{rs}, are to put no more land in tith than is now so, excepting ye Land sown wth clover, and that to lay down ye spring following, and then to lay as much of ye said premises wth clover instead of that parcel of Land, wch shall be plowed and sown in its course, provided also y^t it shall not be lawful for him or them to break up any fresh ground under ye penalty of five pounds p acre, or to take above two crops without making a clean summerley of ye Lands, that now are or shall be in Tith that year when he or they shall leave the premises, being then to be allowed and paid fifteen shillings for every acre so left, and half a crown for every earth-tilling, and to give it three earths, if required.

And ye said Richd Britin for himself, his heirs, and Ex^{rs}, doth covenant and agree not to cut down any wood or bushes, only bushes for necessary fencing, and such wood or bushes as shall be annually set out for firing to ye value of one pound and fifteen shillings ; or in lieu of ye said wood for firing, to have ye said sum of one pound and fifteen shillings paid him by discount of so much in his next half year's rent, as likewise not to let any of ye premises without consent of ye said Philip Williams, nor to sell any of ye Hay, clover, muck, or compost, arising from ye said premises, but to spend ye same upon them, excepting ye crop of that year in wch he or they shall quit ye premises. Provided likewise y^t ye Rev^d Mr. Stillingfleet and ye said Philip Williams and his assigns, shall have ye full use of ye two Parlours, of ye two best Chambers, and of one of ye Garrets, and of such other apartments in ye premises as he or they shall occasion for, provided lastly y^t ye above-named Richd Britin, his Ex^{rs} and Adm^{rs}, shall, from time to time, board and entertain ye Rev^d Mr. Stillingfleet, or ye Curate for ye time being, upon reasonable terms, and shall likewise give free ingress and egress into and from ye said premises at all times to ye above-named Philip Williams, as often as he shall think proper, to repair to and continue in ye said Parsonage House, upon allowing what shall be reasonable for his own and servants' Diet, and for ye corn and provender of his horses.

It is finally stipulated between ye abovewritten parties, yt all repairs, glass windows excepted, belonging to ye house outhouses and walls and gates shall be made good and discharged by ye above-named Philip Williams, and all other repairs and fences whatever to be made good and discharged by yᵉ before-named Richᵈ Britin, his heirs, exʳˢ and admʳˢ, wood and bushes being allowed him for yᵉ same.

In witness whereof the Parties above named have interchangeably set their hands yᵉ day and year above written.

Philip Williams.

Signed in yᵉ presence of Richard Britin.

F. Stillingfleet,
Jeremiah Valiant.

Memorandum.   Notwithstanding the within-written agreement I promise to pay yᵉ window-tax and poor-rate, and to look upon turnips to be no crop.

Philip Williams.

Jan. 1, 1732.

And likewise I promise yt yᵉ within-written Richard Britin after the three years expired, if he shall then leave yᵉ farm, shall have yᵉ liberty of yᵉ Barn to thresh out his corn till yᵉ Lady Day next ensuing.

Philip Williams.

APPENDIX.

I have endeavoured, but I am sorry to say unsuccessfully, to obtain any further information about the chalice. Mr. Manning, our Rural Dean, writes, "I am afraid it is impossible to say now how Archbishop Sancroft became possessed of his Elizabethan cup; but I think there is nothing improbable in its having belonged to the Sancroft family from the first, as they had a house in Fressingfield, where he was born in 1616. He may have had it with him at Lambeth, and have brought it back again. The fact of its not being hall-marked looks as if it was not bought at a shop, but made to order. I might ask Dr. Raven if it is known whether the house had a chapel in Elizabethan times; but even if not, there might have been good reasons in those days for having a private communion set." I wrote to Dr. Raven, and received this answer from him :—
"The Archbishop had a private chapel at Ufford, ...; but I should consider it very doubtful if there had been a chapel there before his return in 1691. There was a chapel at Whittingham in the middle ages, for the font remains in Saml. Cluttens' garden ; but Whittingham was a big place, and the Ufford assessment was not large—ever large enough, I should say, to have afforded this luxury. The family attended Fressingfield or Withersdale. Dr.

William Sandcroft (*sic*), Master of Emmanuel, the Archbishop's uncle, was baptised at Withersdale."

Ufford and Whittingham are old manor houses at Fressingfield. I have asked the librarians at the Lambeth Palace Library, and the Bodleian Library at Oxford, if they could kindly throw any light on my point, but both write regretting very much that they are unable to do so. The Archbishop left all his property, by will, to his nephews, Francis and William: the latter was his steward at Lambeth, but Francis was father to William Sancroft, who married Miss Catherine Cotton, who gave us the chalice, whence we easily see how she became possessed of it.

For the present, then, any history the chalice may have had must remain undecided.

.

www.ingramcontent.com/pod-product-compliance
Lightning Source LLC
Chambersburg PA
CBHW021526270326
41930CB00008B/1109